ON ONE FLOWER

Butterflies, Ticks and a Few More Icks

By Anthony D. Fredericks

Illustrated by Jennifer DiRubbio

Dawn Publications

For my granddaughter Isabelle: May her life be filled with fantastic adventures, magical discoveries and worlds of wonder! — ADF

To my sisters and brothers (through birth and through marriage): Thank you for always being there for me. Your friendship and encouragement mean more to me than you could ever know. — JDR

A Sharing Nature With Children Book

Library of Congress Cataloging-in-Publication Data

Fredericks, Anthony D.
  On one flower : butterflies, ticks, and a few more icks / by Anthony D. Fredericks ;
  Illustrated by Jennifer DiRubbio.
     p. cm.
  Summary: "A child finds a goldenrod flower and, looking closely, discovers a whole community of insects on it. Includes "field notes" of facts about these animals and their relationships, plus resources for further study"--Provided by publisher.
  Includes bibliographical references and index.
  ISBN 1-58469-086-0 (hardback : alk. paper) -- ISBN 1-58469-087-9 (pbk. : alk. paper)
  1. Insects--Juvenile literature. I. DiRubbio, Jennifer, ill. II. Title.
  QL467.2.F74 2006
  595.7--dc22
                            2006000034

Dawn Publications
12402 Bitney Springs Road
Nevada City, CA 95959
530-274-7775
nature@dawnpub.com

Printed in China

10 9 8 7 6 5 4 3 2 1
First Edition

Design and computer production by Patty Arnold, Menagerie Design and Publishing

Dear Friends:

Hey, you stink! Has anyone said that to you? That's what they say to me! You see, when I'm disturbed by a predator I sometimes stink up the neighborhood. Whew! But, that's how I protect myself from critters who would have me for dinner (and I don't mean that they invited me to dinner, either).

I live in an exciting place—an open field. In fact, one of my favorite spots is a goldenrod flower. Here, butterflies fly in and out, caterpillars crawl up and down, and spiders are always hanging around. This is our little community—a neighborhood of friends and foes, residents and visitors.

You can find communities of animals just like us near where you live, too. Just get on your hands and knees, look carefully at a plant or bush, and you may discover a wonderful world right in front of you. You don't need to go to a zoo to find lots of animals living together (besides, zoo animals are big and hairy!). You can discover your own special zoo close to your home or whenever you go on a trip. So, get out and explore . . . and I'll promise not to stink you up—well, not too much!

Your smelly friend,

Stinkbug

This is a field of grasses and trees,
  Where butterflies dance on the afternoon breeze,
With bug-buggy critters that wiggle and creep,
  And silk-spinning spiders who jiggle and leap.
This is where, on warm breezy days,
  A tall yellow flower bobbles and sways.

This is the **flower**.

Two curious boys were wandering by,
Observing the field and the late summer sky.
"I wonder who lives here," one boy did say.
"What could we find on this sunshiny day?"

The boys saw some creatures, some active, some not,
  All living close on this flowery spot.
So they sat on the ground and with eyes open wide,
  They peeked and they peered and they searched and they spied.

This is the **stinkbug**—an animal gross
  (A smell-smelly critter if you get too close).
Upon the tall flower, on a day warm and bright,
  Clings a cluster of neighbors—a startling sight!

A long-legged **spider** is waiting for prey,
  Hiding and searching for bugs the whole day.
Yet he won't grab the stinkbug—an animal gross
  (A smell-smelly critter if you get too close).
Upon the tall flower, on a day warm and bright,
  Clings a cluster of neighbors—a startling sight!

An orange **butterfly** with wings edged in black,
  Glides to the flower and looks for a snack—
Too quick for the spider waiting for prey,
  Who's hiding and searching for bugs the whole day.
Yet he won't grab the stinkbug—an animal gross
  (A smell-smelly critter if you get too close).
All on a tall flower, on a day warm and bright,
  Clings a cluster of neighbors —a startling sight!

A buzz-buzzing **bee** is next to arrive,
  Where she gathers some pollen to take to her hive.
And then comes a butterfly with wings edged in black,
  Who glides to the flower and looks for a snack—
Too quick for the spider waiting for prey,
  Who's hiding and searching for bugs the whole day.
Yet he won't grab the stinkbug—an animal gross
  (A smell-smelly critter if you get too close).
All on a tall flower, on a day warm and bright,
  Clings a cluster of neighbors—a startling sight!

A wandering **ladybug** with spots on her back,
  Hunts for some aphids—an unplanned attack!
A buzz-buzzing bee is next to arrive,
  Where she gathers some pollen to take to her hive.
And then comes a butterfly with wings edged in black,
  Who glides to the flower and looks for a snack—
Too quick for the spider waiting for prey,
  Who's hiding and searching for bugs the whole day.
Yet he won't grab the stinkbug—an animal gross
  (A smell-smelly critter if you get too close).
All on a tall flower, on a day warm and bright,
  Clings a cluster of neighbors—a startling sight!

Hidden and lurking with quick grabbing feet—
   Look out! An **ambush bug**, ready to eat!
Who's eyeing a ladybug with spots on her back,
   Who hunts for some aphids—an unplanned attack!
A buzz-buzzing bee is next to arrive,
   Where she gathers some pollen to take to her hive.
And then comes a butterfly with wings edged in black,
   Who glides to the flower and looks for a snack—
Too quick for the spider waiting for prey,
   Who's hiding and searching for bugs the whole day.
Yet he won't grab the stinkbug—an animal gross
   (A smell-smelly critter if you get too close).
All on a tall flower, on a day warm and bright,
   Clings a cluster of neighbors—a startling sight!

An eight-legged **tick** with a sensitive feel,
　Waits on the stalk for a blood-sucking meal,
Away from the bug with quick-grabbing feet!
　Who lurks in the flower for something eat,
Who's eyeing a ladybug with spots on her back,
　Who hunts for some aphids—an unplanned attack!
A buzz-buzzing bee is next to arrive,
　Where she gathers some pollen to take to her hive.
And then comes the butterfly with wings edged in black,
　Who glides to the flower and looks for a snack—
Too quick for the spider waiting for prey,
　Who's hiding and searching for bugs the whole day.
Yet he won't grab the stinkbug—an animal gross
　(A smell-smelly critter if you get too close).
All on a tall flower, on a day warm and bright,
　Clings a cluster of neighbors—a startling sight!

A medley of creatures inhabits this space,
 A most active flower—a hip-hopping place!
Leaves, petals, and stems: it's where animals thrive
 And each does its best to compete and survive.

Field Notes

In most states and provinces there are prairies, pastures and fields filled with an incredible variety of animal life. Some of the most interesting creatures are the smallest residents. Many of these animals live together in an ecological niche (a small community of animals in a specific area)—a single flower, for example. Some critters are permanent residents and some are just occasional visitors. The creatures in this book can all be found throughout North America.

Goldenrod

Stinkbug

Spider

Butterfly

Goldenrod flowers grow in fields, in woods or along stream banks across North America. There are more than 100 different varieties. All goldenrods have clusters of bright yellow flowers that appear in August and September. The flowers are on long stalks—with some species reaching a height of about six feet. Contrary to popular belief, goldenrod does not cause hay fever. Goldenrods are important to animals such as insects. Here they lay their eggs, hunt for prey, drink nectar, eat leaves and stems, suck plant juices and collect pollen.

Fantastic Fact: The goldenrod is the state flower of two different states: Nebraska and Kentucky.

Stinkbugs are common visitors to many plants—sucking juices from leaves, flowers, fruits, and stems. Most stinkbugs are herbivorous (plant-eaters); however, there are some carnivorous (meat-eating) species. All stinkbugs have a very disagreeable odor that helps protect them from their enemies, which include birds, toads, spiders and other insect-eating animals. The odor comes from two glands on the thorax. The Green Stinkbug is bright green with yellow, orange or red edges. They usually grow to about 3/4" long and in the shape of a tiny shield.

Fantastic Fact: There are more than 5,000 species of stinkbugs throughout the world, with about 500 species in the U.S. alone.

There are more than 35,000 species of spiders throughout the world, including about 3,000 species in North America. All spiders have four pairs of legs and fangs that are used to paralyze or kill their victims, which include bees, butterflies, flies and grasshoppers. The Goldenrod Spider is part of a family of spiders known as crab spiders. These spiders hold their legs out to the sides just like crabs. Goldenrod Spiders live throughout North America—their color often changes to yellow, which camouflages them on goldenrod flowers and yellow daisies.

Fantastic Fact: Like many species of spiders, Goldenrod Spiders have eight eyes arranged in two rows of four eyes each.

The Painted Lady Butterfly can be found in flowery meadows and fields. It may be the most widespread butterfly in the entire world. Besides North America, it also lives throughout Africa, Asia and Europe. Its wings are mostly orange and black with several white spots. The wings also have blue spots along with olive, white and rose-colored patterns. It feeds on the nectar from a wide variety of flowers including goldenrod, aster and mallow. The number of Painted Lady Butterflies in an area is often determined by the number of flowers, the number of parasites, or the amount of winter rainfall. Their enemies include various spiders and other insect-eating predators.

Fantastic Fact: Painted Lady Butterflies, just like all butterflies, taste with their feet.

Honeybee

One of the world's most familiar insects, the honeybee is also one of the most celebrated. People everywhere love the taste of honey and it is because of the tireless work of this insect that this sweet delicacy is available throughout the world. Honeybees usually live in hollow trees or in special hives kept by beekeepers. The workers of a honeybee colony visit many different kinds of flowers in fields, meadows and pastures to gather pollen from which they make honey. A single colony may consist of nearly 100,000 members.

Fantastic Fact: Honeybees will visit about two million flowers and fly approximately 50,000 miles in order to make one pound of honey.

Ladybug

Ladybugs, or ladybird beetles as they are called in England, are very familiar insects. There are more than 4,500 species in the world, but the Two-Spotted Ladybug is found throughout North America. Ladybugs live their lives in two stages. After they hatch from eggs they are called larvae. Larvae may eat up to 300 tiny insects (such as aphids) in a single day. After spending a lot of time eating, they form a cocoon and grow into an adult. Adult ladybugs weigh less than 1/100th of an ounce. Both adults and larvae are predators—primarily hunting and eating aphids and other soft small insects.

Fantastic Fact: Ladybugs are practically blind. They survive only by walking around and bumping into their prey. Then they stop and eat.

Ambush Bug

Ambush bugs are the masters of camouflage. They are usually greenish-yellow or brown and yellow in color. This allows them to hide out in the petals of many different varieties of flowers, including goldenrods. Although they are small (3/8" to 1/2") they are savage attackers, often grabbing insects much larger than themselves (bees, wasps, butterflies and moths). Ambush bugs then immobilize their victims by injecting saliva through their short piercing beaks.

Fantastic Fact: Ambush bugs often attack honeybees and for that reason they are considered to be a pest by beekeepers.

Tick

Ticks have eight legs and a flat body. They cannot fly; they can only crawl. After hatching, a tick crawls up a blade of grass, twig or plant stem and waits. When a warm-blooded animal (such as a deer, dog, or squirrel) passes by, the tick senses the carbon dioxide exhaled by that animal. It then leaps onto the animal. It scuttles beneath the fur or hair of its host and buries the front part of its head into the skin. The tick feeds on the victim's blood until it is full. Then it drops off and digests its meal.

Fantastic Fact: A tick can survive without food for a very long time—months, years, or even decades. This is known as questing behavior.

Dear Reader,

Ecology is the study of animals and the environments in which they live. Here are some of my favorite books about ecology—especially insects, spiders, bugs and other things in nature.

Anthology for the Earth (1998) edited by Judy Allen, a wonderful collection of art, essays and poetry about the planet Earth.

Bugs (1997) by David T. Greenberg, a very humorous (and very gross) poem about all kinds of insects and bugs.

Least Things: Poems About Small Natures (2003) by Jane Yolen, a delightful assembly of short poems about caterpillars, grasshoppers, butterflies and other small things in nature.

Making the World (1998) by Douglas Wood, one of my all-time favorite books about how all creatures (including humans) are important in the world.

Plantzilla (2002) by Jerdine Nolen, a humorous story about a very weird plant and some very strange adventures one summer.

Spiders: Biggest! Littlest! (2004) by Sandra Markle, this book has just about everything you would ever want to know about the spiders of the world.

What to Do When a Bug Climbs in Your Mouth (1995) by Rick Walton, a collection of funny poetry about centipedes, grasshoppers and other buggy critters.

Who is the World For? (2000) by Tom Pow, a magical book that celebrates the importance of everyday pleasures in nature—for animals and humans.

Here are some of the other children's books I've written.

Near One Cattail: Turtles, Logs and Leaping Frogs (2005), an adventure of many sights as a young girl discovers the variety of wildlife in a wetlands area. (2006 Skipping Stones Honor Award and 2006 Green Earth Children's Book Award).

Around One Cactus: Owls, Bats and Leaping Rats (2003), a fun-filled book about the incredible variety of animal life that lives in and around a saguaro cactus (2004 IRA Teacher's Choice Award).

In One Tidepool: Crabs, Snails and Salty Tails (2002), an engaging story about a young girl and her discoveries in a tidepool on a rocky shore.

Under One Rock: Bugs, Slugs and Other Ughs (2001), a rhythmic description of the colorful creatures that live together beneath a single rock (2002 Learning Magazine Teacher's Choice Award).

Zebras (2001), delightful information and amazing photographs about these wonderful creatures.

Slugs (2000), amazing information and incredible photographs about a greatly misunderstood creature (2001 NSTA/CBC Outstanding Science Trade Book).

Here are the names and addresses of organizations working to protect and preserve various ecosystems and animal habitats throughout North America. You may want to contact them to find out what they are doing and how you can become involved.

National Audubon Society
700 Broadway
New York, NY 10003
www.audubon.org

National Wildlife Federation
11100 Wildlife Center Drive
Reston, VA 20190
www.nwf.org

Nature Conservancy
1815 North Lynn Street
Arlington, VA 22209
www.nature.org

World Wildlife Fund
1250 24th Street, NW
Washington, DC
www.panda.org

Young Entomologists' Society
6907 W. Grand River Ave.
Lansing, MI 48906
www.members.aol.com/yesbugs

If you or your teacher would like to learn more about me, the books I write, or the school visits I make, please log on to my web site, www.afredericks.com.

Anthony Fredericks is a veteran nature explorer. He grew up on the beaches of southern California and during summers camped (and swatted mosquitoes) in the Sierra Nevada mountains of eastern California. Later he attended high school and college in Arizona where he often spent his free time trekking through the Sonoran desert. Now Tony explores the hillside in south-central Pennsylvania where he and his wife reside and frequently hikes the mountains of western Colorado where his granddaughter lives. A former classroom teacher and reading specialist, he is Professor of Education at York College. As the author of more than 30 children's books (some about "buggy" things) he is a frequent visitor to schools around the country, where he shares the wonders of nature with a new generation of naturalists.

Photo by Erika Kuciw

Jennifer DiRubbio is both a passionate artist and an avid environmentalist. She has been active as an artist for several organizations that promote nature and a healthy planet. Jennifer graduated with a BFA from Pratt Institute in 1992. She keeps her home and studio in Merrick, New York, as "green" and environmentally sound as possible, where her husband and two young children also work and play.

OTHER BOOKS BY
ANTHONY FREDERICKS AND JENNIFER DIRUBBIO

Under One Rock: Bugs, Slugs and Other Ughs. A whole community of creatures lives under rocks. No child will be able to resist taking a peek after reading this.

In One Tidepool: Crabs, Snails and Salty Tails. Have you ever ventured to the edge of the sea and peered into a tidepool? A colorful community of creatures lives there!

Around One Cactus: Owls, Bats and Leaping Rats. A saguaro cactus may look lonely, standing in the dry, dry desert—but it is a haven for creatures, both cute and creepy!

Near One Cattail: Turtles, Logs and Leaping Frogs. What creatures live in a bog-boggy place? Many—and they swim, soar and crawl!

A FEW OTHER NATURE AWARENESS TITLES FROM DAWN PUBLICATIONS

The Web at Dragonfly Pond by Brian "Fox" Ellis, illustrated by Michael S. Maydak. A true tale of fishing with father that gives a whole new insight on a child's place in the web of life.

Eliza and the Dragonfly by Susie Caldwell Rinehart, illustrated by Anisa Claire Hovemann. Almost despite herself, Eliza becomes entranced by the "awful" dragonfly nymph—and before long, both of them are transformed.

Earth Day, Birthday by Pattie Schnetzler, illustrated by Chad Wallace. To the tune of "The Twelve Days of Christmas," here is a sing-along, read-along book that honors the animals, the environment, and a universal holiday all in one fresh approach.

City Beats: A Hip-Hoppy Pigeon Poem, by S. Kelly Rammell, illustrated by Jeanette Canyon. From a pigeon's-eye view, a city is a marvelous place.

Dawn Publications is dedicated to inspiring in children a deeper understanding and appreciation for all life on Earth. To review our titles or to order, please visit us at www.dawnpub.com, or call 800-545-7475.